Cooper
What is that?

By Sarah Edmondson

Cooper asks his friends "what is that?"

 @rhodesian_ridgeback_cooper

www.ingramcontent.com/pod-product-compliance
Lightning Source LLC
Chambersburg PA
CBHW041232040426
42444CB00002B/140